D1995650

Thai for Beginners

The Ultimate Thai Language

Software

PAIBOON PUBLISHING

Thai for Beginners (The Ultimate Thai Language) Software

Copyright ©2004 by Paiboon Publishing
(สำนักพิมพ์ไพบูลย์ภูมิแสน)
Printed in Thailand
All rights reserved

Paiboon Poomsan Publishing
582 Amarinniwate Village 2
Nawamin 90 (Sukhapiban 1)
Bungkum, Bangkok 10230
THAILAND
☎ 662-509-8632
Fax 662-519-5437

Paiboon Publishing
PMB 192, 1442A Walnut Street
Berkeley, California USA 94709
☎ 1-510-848-7086
Fax 1-510-848-4521

info@paiboonpublishing.com
www.paiboonpublishing.com

สำนักพิมพ์ไพบูลย์ภูมิแสน
582 หมู่บ้านอัมรินทร์นิเวศน์ 2
ถ. นวมินทร์ 90 (สุขา 1) เขตบึงกุ่ม
ก.ท.ม. 10230
☎ 662-509-8632
โทรสาร 662-519-5437

info@paiboonpublishing.com
www.paiboonpublishing.com

Graphic Designers:
Randy Kincaid and Tanapong Praphantanathorn
Speakers:
Benjawan Becker, Adissapong Praphantanathorn and Chayan Chantawongsatorn
Programmer: Dominique Mayrand

ISBN 1-887521-41-0

WELCOME

ยินดีต้อนรับ

Thank you for purchasing **Thai for Beginners** The Ultimate Thai Language **Software** or **TFBS**.

Thai for Beginners Software runs on the following operating systems: Windows 98, ME, 2000 and XP.

Your TFBS serial number is...

PPTHB-0100-RS-01062221

Please respect our copyright by not duplicating this product. Allow us to continue producing quality software for your future learning.

กรุณาอย่าก๊อปปี้ซอฟแวร์ของเรา กว่าจะผลิตสินค้าชิ้นนี้ออกมาได้
ทีมงานของเราต้องเหน็ดเหนื่อยมาก เราหวังว่าจะมีโอกาส
และกองทุนในการสร้างสินค้าที่มีคุณภาพเพื่อรับใช้ท่านอีกในอนาคต

Installation Procedures

Insert Thai for Beginners Software CD into the CD-ROM drive.

If the Setup does not start automatically then click "Run" from the "Start" menu and type: "D:\Setup.exe" (where "D:" is the location of your CD-ROM drive).

Press Enter and complete the Setup. This may take several minutes.

Once the TFBS installation is complete you must run another Setup. For this you must run the "D:\InstallRedist.bat" file located on TFBS CD.

Follow the installation procedure for DirectX. Once the installation is completed you will need to reboot your machine. You are now ready to run Thai for Beginners Software.

Table of Contents

Introduction

Thai for Beginners Software is designed both for people who are just starting to study the Thai language for the first time and for those who want to improve their basic Thai. It teaches the basic language skills—speaking, and, reading and some writing. The first part of each lesson teaches vocabulary and sentence structure and includes a vocabulary list with Thai spelling, transliteration and definitions in English.

The transliteration system assists you with pronunciation while you are learning the Thai alphabet. You can turn the phonetic transliteration display on or off. It's important that you learn to properly pronounce the tones and sounds of Thai. Although Thai for Beginners Software is written with self-study in mind, a Thai teacher or tutor should listen to and correct your pronunciation, especially at the beginning.

We encourage beginning students of Thai to learn the alphabet. Even though conversation may be your principal goal, the Thai alphabet is quite phonetic and studying it will reinforce speaking and listening skills as well as reading and writing. Wean yourself off of transliteration as soon as possible. You won't regret the extra effort spent learning the Thai writing system. For a more comprehensive writing system, please refer to the book "Thai for Beginners" by Paiboon Publishing.

Characteristics of the Thai language different from English include:

- ❑ There are no variant or plural forms for adjectives and nouns.
- ❑ Adjectives follow the noun. In Thai we say, "car white" instead of "white car".
- ❑ There are no verb conjugations in Thai. Tenses are understood from the context or from adverbs of time.
- ❑ There are no articles (a, an, the).
- ❑ There is no verb 'to be' with adjectives. "You're beautiful" would be "You beautiful".
- ❑ There are ending particles that imply the needs, age, social status and feelings of the speaker.
- ❑ Classifiers are used with virtually all nouns.
- ❑ Thai usually omits the subject of a sentence when it is understood from the context.
- ❑ Thai is a tonal language.
- ❑ If the tone is not correct, you won't be easily understood, even if your pronunciation is otherwise perfect.

Please note that the male and female speakers say exactly the same thing, except the male speaker uses "pǒm" for 'I' and the female speaker uses "di-chán" or "chán". You should also add the ending polite particles when appropriate: "kráp" for men and "kâ" or "ká" for women.

This Thai language learning software can be used in combination with our Thai-English, English-Thai Dictionary for Non-Thai Speakers to expand your vocabulary and language usage.

We hope you enjoy this language course in the software format and are certain you will find it fun and worthwhile to communicate with the Thai people in their own language.

Guide to Pronunciation

Tones

Because Thai is a tonal language, its pronunciation presents new challenges for English speakers. If the tone is wrong, you will not be easily understood even if everything else is correct. Thai uses five tones. For example, to pronounce a rising tone, your voice starts at a low pitch and goes up (much like asking a question in English). The phonetic transliteration in this text book uses tone marks over the vowels to show the tone for each word. Note that the tone marks used for transliteration are different from those used in Thai script.

Tone Marks (Transliteration)

Tone	Tone symbol	Example
mid	*None*	maa
low	`	màa
falling	^	mâa
high	´	máa
rising	ˇ	mǎa

Vowels

Most Thai vowels have two versions, short and long. Short vowels are clipped and cut off at the end. Long ones are drawn out. This book shows short vowels with a single letter and long vowels with double letters ('a' for short; 'aa' for long).

The 'ʉ' has no comparable sound in English. Try saying 'u' while spreading your lips in as wide a smile as possible. If the sound you are making is similar to one you might have uttered after stepping on something disgusting, you are probably close!

Short & Long Vowels

a	*like a in Alaska*	fan - *teeth*
aa	*like a in father*	maa - *come*
i	*like i in tip*	sìp - *ten*
ii	*like ee in see*	sìi - *four*
u	*like oo in boot*	kun - *you*
uu	*like u in ruler*	sǔun - *zero*
ʉ	*like u in ruler, but with a smile*	nʉ̀ng - *one*
ʉʉ	*like ʉ but longer*	mʉʉ - *hand*
e	*like e in pet*	sèt - *finish*
ee	*like a in pale*	pleeng-*song*
ε	*like a in cat*	lέ - *and*
εε	*like a in sad*	dεεng - *red*

ə	*like er in teacher without the* r *sound*	lə́ - *dirty*
əə	*like ə but longer*	jəə - *meet*
o	*like o in note*	jon - *poor*
oo	*like o in go*	joon -*robber*
ɔ	*like au in caught*	gɔ̀ - *island*
ɔɔ	*like aw in law*	nɔɔn - *sleep*

Complex Vowels

The following dipthongs are combinations of the above vowels.

ai	mâi - *not*	aai	saai - *sand*
ao	mao - *drunk*	aao	kâao - *rice*
ia	bia - *beer*	iao	nǐao - *sticky*
ua	dtua- *body*	uai	ruai - *rich*
ʉa	rʉa - *boat*	ʉai	nʉ̀ai - *tired*
ɔi	nɔ̀i - *little*	ɔɔi	kɔɔi - *wait*
ooi	dooi - *by*	əəi	nəəi - *butter*
ui	kui - *chat*	iu	hǐu - *hungry*
eo	reo - *fast*	eeo	eeo - *waist*
ɛo	tɛ̌o - *row*	ɛɛo	lɛ́ɛo - *already*

Consonants

b	*as in baby*	bin - *fly*
ch	*as in chin*	chûu - *name*
d	*as in doll*	duu - *look*
f	*as in fun*	fai - *fire*
g	*as in gold*	gin - *eat*
h	*as in honey*	hâa - *five*
j	*as in jet*	jèt - *seven*
k	*as in kiss*	kon - *person*
l	*as in love*	ling - *monkey*
m	*as in money*	mii - *have*
n	*as in need*	naa - *rice field*
p	*as in pretty*	pan - *thousand*
r	*rolled like the Spanish r*	rian - *study*
s	*as in sex*	sìi - *four*
t	*as in tender*	tam - *do*
w	*as in woman*	wan - *day*
y	*as in you*	yaa - *medicine*
ng	*as in ringing*	ngaan - *work*
dt	*as in stop*	dtaa - *eye*
bp	*as in spot*	bpai - *go*
gw	*as in Guam*	gwàa - *more than*
kw	*as in queer*	kwaam - *matter*

Practice saying the words below while your teacher listens. Then have your teacher say the words and see if you can hear the tones correctly.

Mid	**Low**	**Falling**	**High**	**Rising**
maa *to come*	-	-	máa *horse*	mǎa *dog*
mai *mile*	mài *new*	mâi *no, not*	mái *....., right?*	mǎi *silk*
glai *far*	-	glâi *near*	-	-
sai *fish trap*	sài *to wear*	sâi *intestine*	sái *to preen*	sǎi *clear*
paa *to take*	pàa *to split*	pâa *cloth*	-	pǎa *cliff*
kaao *fishy*	kàao *news*	kâao *rice*	-	kǎao *white*
-	wàt *a cold*	-	wát *temple*	-
-	sʉ̀a *mat*	sʉ̂a *shirt*	-	sʉ̌a *tiger*
yaa *medicine*	yàa *"don't"*	yâa *grandmother, grass*	-	-

Practice the Following Words

A. Words with mid tones:

1.	dii	ดี	*good*
2.	kon	คน	*person*
3.	jai	ใจ	*heart*
4.	aai	อาย	*to be shy*
5.	kruu	ครู	*teacher*

B. Words with low tones:

1.	nʉ̀ng	หนึ่ง	*one*
2.	sìi	สี่	*four*
3.	jèt	เจ็ด	*seven*
4.	jà	จะ	*will*
5.	sèt	เสร็จ	*to finish*

C. Words with falling tones:

1.	hâa	ห้า	*five*
2.	gâao	เก้า	*nine*
3.	nîi	นี่	*this*
4.	châi	ใช่	*correct*
5.	mâi	ไม่	*not, no*

D. Words with high tones:

1.	fáa	ฟ้า	*blue, sky*
2.	náam	น้ำ	*water*
3.	chái	ใช้	*to use*
4.	rúu	รู้	*to know*
5.	rák	รัก	*to love*

E. Words with rising tones:

1.	mǎa	หมา	*dog*
2.	sǔung	สูง	*tall*
3.	nǎngsʉ̌ʉ	หนังสือ	*book*
4.	mǔu	หมู	*pig*
5.	kǎao	ขาว	*white*

More About Tones, Short-Long Vowels, Similar Consonants and Vowel Sounds

When you are not understood, often you are saying the tone wrong. However, the length of the vowel is also very important. Try to get the vowel length correct. This will help you to be understood better while you are still learning to master the tones.

Practice saying the following words.

Different Tone, Different Meaning

1.	maa	มา	*to come*
	máa	ม้า	*horse*
	mǎa	หมา	*dog*
2.	mai	ไมล์	*mile*
	mài	ใหม่	*new*
	mâi	ไม่, ไหม้	*no, to burn*
	mái	มั้ย	*....., right?*
	mǎi	ไหม	*silk*
3.	kào	เข่า	*knee*
	kâo	เข้า	*to enter*
	káo	เค้า	*he/she*
	kǎo	เขา	*animal horn, he/she*
4.	kaao	คาว	*fishy*
	kàao	ข่าว	*news*
	kâao	ข้าว	*rice*
	kǎao	ขาว	*white*
5.	sii	ซี	*"a particle"*
	sìi	สี่	*four*
	sîi	ซี่	*the classifier for "tooth"*
	sǐi	สี	*color*

6.	glai	ไกล	*far*
	glâi	ใกล้	*near*
7.	sʉ̀a	เสื่อ	*mat*
	sʉ̂a	เสื้อ	*shirt*
	sʉ̌a	เสือ	*tiger*
8.	baa	บาร์	*bar*
	bàa	บ่า	*shoulder*
	bâa	บ้า	*mad, crazy*
9.	paa	พา	*to take along*
	pàa	ผ่า	*to cut, to split*
	pâa	ผ้า	*cloth*
	pǎa	ผา	*cliff*
10.	bpaa	ปา	*to throw*
	bpàa	ป่า	*forest*
	bpâa	ป้า	*aunt*
	bpǎa	ป๋า	*father (of a Chinese Thai)*
11.	yàak	อยาก	*to want to*
	yâak	ยาก	*difficult*
12.	yaa	ยา	*medicine*
	yàa	อย่า	*don't*
	yâa	ย่า	*grandmother*
13.	bpuu	ปู	*crab*
	bpùu	ปู่	*grandfather*
14.	naa	นา	*rice field*
	nâa	หน้า	*face, season*
	nǎa	หนา	*thick*
15.	mii	มี	*to have*
	mìi	หมี่	*dry noodle*
	mǐi	หมี	*bear*

16.	pѐt	เผ็ด	*spicy*
	pét	เพชร	*diamond*
17.	nai	ใน	*in*
	nǎi	ไหน	*where*
18.	wàt	หวัด	*a cold*
	wát	วัด	*temple*
19.	sai	ไซ	*a kind of fish trap*
	sài	ใส่	*to put on, to wear*
	sâi	ไส้	*intestine*
	sái	ไซ้	*to preen (the feathers)*
	sǎi	ใส	*clear*
20.	saai	ทราย	*sand*
	sàai	ส่าย	*to shake*
	sáai	ซ้าย	*left*
	sǎai	สาย	*late*

Short and Long Vowels

1.	kǎo	เขา	*horn*	kǎao	ขาว	*white*
2.	kâo	เข้า	*to enter*	kâao	ข้าว	*rice*
3.	jan	จันทร์	*moon*	jaan	จาน	*plate*
4.	yang	ยัง	*yet*	yaang	ยาง	*rubber*
5.	kun	คุณ	*you*	kuun	คูณ	*to multiply*
6.	sǎi	ใส	*clear*	sǎai	สาย	*late*
7.	mâi	ไม่	*no*	mâai	ม่าย	*widower*
8.	jàk	จักร	*sewing machine*	jàak	จาก	*from*
9.	nai	ใน	*in*	naai	นาย	*Mr.*
10.	rao	เรา	*we*	raao	ราว	*about*

Similar Sounds

1.	dii	ดี	*good*	dtii	ตี	*to hit*
2.	bai	ใบ	*leaf*	bpai	ไป	*to go*
3.	nǔu	หนู	*mouse*	nguu	งู	*snake*
4.	pèt	เผ็ด	*spicy*	bpèt	เป็ด	*duck*
5.	tǔng	ถุง	*bag*	tʉ̌ng	ถึง	*to*
6.	krʉ̂ang	เครื่อง	*machine*	krʉ̂ng	ครึ่ง	*half*
7.	dao	เดา	*to guess*	dtao	เตา	*stove*
8.	nəən	เนิน	*mound, hill*	ngən	เงิน	*money*
9.	ùut	อูฐ	*camel*	ʉ̀ut	อืด	*swollen*
10.	glua	กลัว	*to be afraid*	glʉa	เกลือ	*salt*

Irregular Tones

The tone pronunciation of some common words has evolved and they are now usually pronounced differently from the way they are written in Thai script. For example:

ดิฉัน (dì-chǎn) is usually pronounced ดิชั้น (dì-chán).
เขา (kǎo) is usually pronounced เค้า (káo).
ไหม (mǎi) (the particle) is usually pronounced มั้ย (mái).

In our transliteration system, we give the pronunciation most commonly used by modern Thai speakers. For example:

ดิฉัน is transcribed as dì-chán. เขา is transcribed as káo.
ไหม is transcribed as mái.

For poly-syllabic words, in normal speech, the tone of the initial syllable tends to become a mid tone. For example:

à-rai sounds like a-rai in normal speech.
sà-wàtdii sounds like sa-wàtdii in normal speech.

Thai for Beginners Software User's Manual

1. Welcome

Thank you for purchasing Thai for Beginners – The Ultimate Thai Language Software (TFB or Thai for Beginners Software). We hope that you will find this software learning tool to be user-friendly and enjoyable.

TFB has over 3700 voice recordings along with customizable Thai script and phonetic transliteration. You can also select between male or female speakers for all entries to help you improve your listening skills.

2. Requirements

2.1. OS

TFBS works on the following operating systems:
Windows 98, Windows ME, Windows 2000 and Windows XP.

It is recommended that you have the most recent service pack of the OS you are using before installing TFBS.

2.2 Hardware Requirements

Requirements:

- ❑ Pentium PIII 500 Mhz
- ❑ 100% DirectX compatible Sound card
- ❑ At least 64 megs of memory for Windows 98/ME and at least 128 megs for Windows 2000/XP
- ❑ At least 120 megabytes of free hard disk space

3. Installation

3.1 Installation Requirements

Before installing, you must have the following component already installed on your computer:

Microsoft Internet Explorer 5.01 or greater.

3.2 Installation Procedures

Put the Thai for Beginners Software CD ROM into your CD ROM drive. If the Setup does not start automatically then click "Run" from the "Start" menu and type: "D:\Setup.exe" (where "D:" is the location of your CD-ROM drive). Press Enter and complete the Setup. This may take several minutes.

Once the TFBS installation is complete you must run another Setup. For this you must run the "D:\InstallRedist.bat" file located on TFBS CD. Follow the installation procedure for DirectX. Once the installation is completed you will need to reboot your machine. You are now ready to run Thai for Beginners Software.

4. Thai for Beginners Software Overview

Once installed, Thai for Beginners Software can be found in the Start menu under “Paiboon Publishing”. When starting the TFBS, you should hear music. If no music is heard, first check your hardware, then check if you have installed DirectX 9 Manager properly.

4.1 Lesson Dialog

Lesson Dialog is the Main Application Dialog. From there you can:

- ❑ Go to Configuration Dialog
- ❑ Go to About Dialog
- ❑ Go to Exercise Selection Dialog
- ❑ Start a Test
- ❑ Close Thai for Beginners Software

4.2 Configuration Dialog

Configuration Dialog can be started from the main application dialog.

Reading Tab

Thai Fonts

In the configuration dialog you can change the Thai fonts that will be displayed during the Exercise and the Introduction. You can customize a font size that can be easily readable for you.

International Phonetic Alphabet Check Box

The International Phonetic Alphabet (IPA) is most useful for beginners to help them with pronunciation of the Thai language. If you are not familiar with the Thai alphabet, you should use this option. IPA transliteration should be used as reference only. Once you start become familiar with the Thai alphabet, we suggest that you try to read the Thai script only and turn off the IPA.

Voices Tab

Two choices of speakers, male or female, are available. This feature is useful for you to get accustomed to different speakers. You can select one gender (either the male or female) and later switch to the other when you wish, or use the "Random" setting in which you will hear male or female speakers randomly chosen by the program.

4.3 About Dialog

The about dialog can be displayed from the main dialog.
It displays the product and license information.

4.4 Exercise Selection Dialog

The exercise selection dialog can be displayed from the lesson selection dialog by clicking the "Begin" button.

- ❑ Lessons

  The lesson column displays the "Sub-lessons" associated with that particular lesson.
- ❑ Scores

  The score column displays the score result of the latest exer cise you have completed.

From this dialog, the user has a choice to start an "Introduction" or an "Exercise" for a different lesson. Once the choice has been made, click the "Begin" button.

4.4.1 Introduction Dialog

This dialog lists all of the learning material of the selected "Sub-Lessons". You can read or listen to this material using the control buttons.

4.4.2 Exercise Dialog

With the exercise dialog, you simply have to match the Thai word with its English translation. The length of the exercise depends on the amount of learning material associated with a particular lesson.
It is considered a "false" answer when you click on the wrong English translation. In order to go to the next item, you must have the correct answer.
More information is displayed when you choose the wrong answer. For example, the Thai script for that word will appear and the IPA (if, in the configuration dialog, you have chosen IPA to appear).

If you close this dialog before the end of the exercise, the score will not be saved.

4.5 Results Dialog

This dialog appears after you have completed an exercise or a test. The "Action" panel is not available for a completed test.

5. Start Learning

We suggest that you get acquainted with the Thai Script by learning the Thai Alphabet in Appendix II. If you use the IPA, please refer to the Guide to Pronunciation in this manual, then start the introduction and continue with the lessons. If you have problems viewing the Thai fonts go to the configuration dialog and change the font settings so they are easily readable for you.
Listening Skills:
The more you listen to Thai, the better you will be able to distinguish the tones, the long-short vowels and other difficult sounds. If you have difficulty understanding a word, try switching speakers.

Reading Skills:
First learn the Thai script - consonants and vowels in Appendix II.

6. How to Contact Us

Technical support regarding this product is offered only by email. Allow 3 to 5 days for a reply. We can be reached at: support@paiboon-publishing.com .

To facilitate a fast response, please include the following information in your email :
Name:
Country:
Phone Number:
Serial Number:
Product Name:
Product Version:
Description of the Problem:

Note that all personal data you are sending to us is strictly confidential between you and Paiboon Publishing. We will not publish this information or give it to a third party. It will strictly be used for technical support purposes only.

7. Thai for Beginners Software FAQs

Q. I put the CD in my computer and the setup of Thai for Beginners Software did not start (nothing happens), what should I do to run the setup?

A. If the setup does not start automatically, you must start it manually. In order to do this, open a “Command” window and type:
D:\ Setup.exe..
Replace “D:\” by the letter that reference your CD-ROM drive where TFB is installed then press enter.

Q. When the setup of Thai for Beginners Software starts, I receive a message that "Microsoft .Net Framework" is required in order to run the setup.

How do I install this runtime?

A. "Microsoft .Net Framework" runtime is required on your machine in order to run the Thai for Beginners Software setup and Thai for Beginners Software.

Microsoft .Net Framework setup comes with the Thai for Beginners Software CD and must be manually installed. In order to do this, open a “Command” window and type:
D:\ 3rdParty\DotNetFix\dotnetfx.exe.
Replace “D:\” by the letter that reference your CD-ROM drive where TFB is installed, then press enter.

Q. I have installed successfully Thai for Beginners Software but when I try to start it, it keeps asking me to enter a valid serial number. Where should I get this serial number?

A. The serial number is inside the package on the Getting Started Document. Use this serial number to "unlock" Thai for Beginners Software.

Q. When I start Thai for Beginners Software, I receive an error that Microsoft Data Access Components "MDAC" is not installed and is required. How do I install it?
A. MDAC is provided in the Thai for Beginners Software CD. To run its setup, open a "Command" window and type:
D:\3rdParty\mdac_typ.exe
Replace "D:\" with the letter that references your CD-ROM drive where TFB is installed, then press enter.

Q. When I run Thai for Beginners Software, everything looks fine except when I try to listen to the voice recording. I have an error occurring. What should I do to fix this problem?
A. DirectX 9 is not installed or is not installed properly. To fix this problem, open a "Command" window and type:
D:\ 3rdParty\DX\DXSetupManaged.bat
Replace "D:\" with the letter that references your CD-ROM drive where TFB is installed then press enter.

Q. I receive an error that JET engine is not installed properly. What should I do to fix this problem?
A. To fix this problem, open a "Command" window and type:
D:\ 3rdParty\DX\DXSetupManaged.bat
Replace "D:\" with the letter that references your CD-ROM drive where TFB is installed then press enter.

Q. What are the requirements for installing and running Thai for Beginners Software?
A. The software requirements for the supporting OSs are:

- Microsoft Explorer 6 or higher with high encryption pack (128 bits)
- Microsoft .Net Framework
- Jet Engine
- Microsoft Data Access Components 2.7 (MDAC)
- DirectX 9 (Managed).

Q. What are the Operating Systems Thai for Beginners Software runs on?
A. Thai for Beginners Software runs on the following OSs:
Windows 98, Windows ME, Windows 2000, Windows XP. These OS must have the latest service pack installed. Thai for Beginners Software does not run on Windows NT 4.

Q. If I have other technical problems not listed above, who should I contact?
A. Please email your questions to support@paiboonpublishiing.com.

8. END-USER LICENSE AGREEMENT FOR PAIBOON PUBLISHING SOFTWARE
IMPORTANT—PLEASE READ CAREFULLY.

This End-User License Agreement ("EULA") is a legal agreement between you (either an individual or a single entity) and Paiboon Publishing Incorporated for the Paiboon Publishing software product(s), which includes computer software and may include associated media, printed materials, "online" or electronic documentation, and Internet-based services ("Product"). An amendment or addendum to this EULA may accompany the Product. YOU AGREE TO BE BOUND BY THE TERMS OF THIS EULA BY INSTALLING, COPYING, OR OTHERWISE USING THE PRODUCT. IF YOU DO NOT AGREE, DO NOT INSTALL OR USE THE PRODUCT.

SOFTWARE PRODUCT LICENSE

1. GRANT OF LICENSE. Paiboon Publishing grants you the rights described in this EULA provided that you comply with all terms and conditions of this EULA.

1.1 General License Grant. Paiboon Publishing grants to you as an individual, a personal, nonexclusive license to make and use copies of the Product for the purposes of designing, developing, and testing your software product(s), provided that you are the only individual using the Product.

If you are an entity, Paiboon Publishing grants to you a personal, nonexclusive license to make and use copies of the Product, provided that for each individual using the Product within your organization, you have acquired a separate and valid license for each such individual.

1.2 Documentation. You may make and use an unlimited number of copies of any documentation, provided that such copies shall be used only for personal purposes and are not to be republished or distributed (either in hard copy or electronic form) beyond your premises.

1.3 Storage/Network Use. You may also store or install a copy of the Product on a storage device, such as a network server, used only to install or run the Product on computers used by a licensed end user in accordance with Section 1.1. A single license for the Product may not be shared or used concurrently by other end users.

4. DESCRIPTION OF OTHER RIGHTS AND LIMITATIONS

4.1 Not For Resale Software. If the Product is labeled "Not For Resale" or "NFR," then you may not resell, or otherwise transfer for value, the Product.

4.2 Limitations on Reverse Engineering, Decompilation, and Disassembly. You may not reverse engineer, decompile, or disassemble the Product, except and only to the extent that such activity is expressly permitted by applicable law notwithstanding this limitation.

4.3 Rental. You may not rent, lease or lend the Product.

4.4 Trademarks. This EULA does not grant you any rights in connection with any trademarks or service marks of Paiboon Publishing.

4.5 Consent to Use of Data. You agree that Paiboon Publishing and its affiliates may collect and use technical information gathered as part of the product support services provided to you, if any, related to the Product. Paiboon Publishing may use this information solely to improve our products or to provide customized services or technologies to you and will not disclose this information in a form that personally identifies you.

4.6 Software Transfer. The initial user of the Product may make a one-time permanent transfer of this EULA and Product only directly to an end user. This transfer must include all of the Product (including all component parts, the media and printed materials, any upgrades, this EULA, and, if applicable, the Certificate of Authenticity). Such transfer may not be by way of consignment or any other indirect transfer. The transferee of such one-time transfer must agree to comply with the terms of this EULA, including the obligation not to further transfer this EULA and Product.

4.7 Termination. Without prejudice to any other rights, Paiboon Publishing may terminate this EULA if you fail to comply with the terms and conditions of this EULA. In such event, you must destroy all copies of the Product and all of its component parts.

5. PRERELEASE CODE. Portions of the Product may be identified as prerelease code ("Prerelease Code"). Such Prerelease Code is not at the level of performance and compatibility of the final, generally available product offering. The Prerelease Code may not operate correctly and may be substantially modified prior to first commercial shipment. Paiboon Publishing is not obligated to make this or any later version of the Prerelease Code commercially available. The grant of license to use Prerelease Code expires upon availability of a commercial release of the Prerelease Code from Paiboon Publishing. NOTE: In the event that Prerelease Code contains a separate end-user license agreement, the terms and conditions of such end-user license agreement shall govern your use of the corresponding Prerelease Code.

6. UPGRADES. To use a Product identified as an upgrade, you must first be licensed for the product identified by Paiboon Publishing as eligible for the upgrade. After upgrading, you may no longer use the product that formed the basis for your upgrade eligibility. You may use the resulting upgraded product only in accordance with the terms of this EULA. If the Product is an upgrade of a component of a package of software programs that you licensed as a single product, the Product may be used and transferred only as part of that single product package and may not be separated for use by more than one end user.

7. DOWNGRADES. Instead of installing and using the Product, you may install and use one copy of an earlier version of the Product, provided that you com-

pletely remove such earlier version and install the original Product within a reasonable time. Your use of such earlier version shall be governed by this EULA, and your rights to use such earlier version shall terminate when you install the original Product.

8. DISCLAIMER OF WARRANTIES. To the maximum extent permitted by applicable law, Paiboon Publishing and its suppliers provide to you the PRODUCT, and any (if any) support services relating to the PRODUCT ("Support Services") AS IS AND WITH ALL FAULTS; and Paiboon Publishing and its suppliers hereby disclaim with respect to the Product and Support Services all warranties and conditions, whether express, implied or statutory, including, but not limited to, any (if any) warranties, duties or conditions of or related to: merchantability, fitness for a particular purpose, lack of viruses, accuracy or completeness of responses, results, workmanlike effort and lack of negligence. Also there is no warranty, duty or condition of title, quiet enjoyment, quiet possession, correspondence to description or non-infringement. The entire risk arising out of use or performance of the product and any support services remains with you.

For the limited warranties and special provisions pertaining to your particular jurisdiction, please refer to your warranty booklet included with this package or provided with the software product printed materials.

9. EXCLUSION OF INCIDENTAL, CONSEQUENTIAL AND CERTAIN OTHER DAMAGES. To the maximum extent permitted by applicable law, in no event shall Paiboon Publishing or its suppliers be liable for any special, incidental, punitive, indirect, or consequential damages whatsoever (including, but not limited to, damages for loss of profits or confidential or other information, for business interruption, for personal injury, for loss of privacy, for failure to meet any duty including of good faith or of reasonable care, for negligence, and for any other pecuniary or other loss whatsoever) arising out of or in any way related to the use of or inability to use the product, the provision of or failure to provide support or other services, informaton, software, and related content through the product or otherwise arising out of the use of the product, or otherwise under or in connection with any provision of this EULA, even in the event of the fault, tort (including negligence), strict liability, breach of contract or breach of warranty of Paiboon Publishing or any supplier, and even if Paiboon Publishing or any supplier has been advised of the possibility of such damages. Because some states/jurisdictions do not allow the exclusion or limitation of liability for consequential or incidental damages, the above limitation may not apply to you.

10. LIMITATION OF LIABILITY AND REMEDIES. Notwithstanding any damages that you might incur for any reason whatsoever (including, without limitation, all damages referenced above and all direct or general damages), the entire liability of Paiboon Publishing and any of its suppliers under any provision of this EULA and your exclusive remedy for all of the foregoing (except for any remedy of repair or replacement elected by Paiboon Publishing with respect to any breach of the Limited Warranty) shall be limited to the greater of the amount actually paid by you for the Product or U.S.$5.00. The foregoing limitations, exclusions and disclaimers (including Sections 8 and 9 above) shall apply to the maximum extent permitted by applicable law, even if any remedy fails its essential purpose.

11. LINKS TO THIRD PARTY SITES. You may link to third party sites through the use of the Product. The third party sites are not under the control of Paiboon Publishing, and Paiboon Publishing is not responsible for the contents of any third party sites, any links contained in third party sites, or any changes or updates to third party sites. Paiboon Publishing is not responsible for webcasting or any other form of transmission received from any third party sites. Paiboon Publishing is providing these links to third party sites to you only as a convenience, and the inclusion of any link does not imply an endorsement by Paiboon Publishing of the third party site.

12. U.S. GOVERNMENT LICENSE RIGHTS. All Product provided to the U.S. Government pursuant to solicitations issued on or after December 1, 1995 is provided with the commercial license rights and restrictions described elsewhere herein. All Product provided to the U.S. Government pursuant to solicitations issued prior to December 1, 1995 is provided with "Restricted Rights" as provided for in FAR, 48 CFR 52.227-14 (JUNE 1987) or DFAR, 48 CFR 252.227-7013 (OCT 1988), as applicable.

13. EXPORT RESTRICTIONS. You acknowledge that the Product is of U.S. origin and subject to U.S. export jurisdiction. You agree to comply with all applicable international and national laws that apply to the Product, including the U.S. Export Administration Regulations, as well as end-user, end-use, and destination restrictions issued by U.S. and other governments.

14. APPLICABLE LAW. If you acquired this Product in the United States, this EULA is governed by the laws of the State of California. If this Product was acquired outside the United States, then local law may apply.

15. ENTIRE AGREEMENT. This EULA (including any addendum or amendment to this EULA which is included with the Product) are the entire agreement between you and Paiboon Publishing relating to the Product and the support services (if any) and they supersede all prior or contemporaneous oral or written communications, proposals and representations with respect to the Product or any other subject matter covered by this EULA. To the extent the terms of any Paiboon Publishing policies or programs for support services conflict with the terms of this EULA, the terms of this EULA shall control.

16. The Product is protected by copyright and other intellectual property laws and treaties. Paiboon Publishing or its suppliers own the title, copyright, and other intellectual property rights in the Product. The Product is licensed, not sold.

Please respect our copyright by not duplicating this product. Allow us to continue producing quality software for your future learning. Thank you.

PAIBOON
PUBLISHING

Thai Language Books by Paiboon Publishing

Title: **Thai for Beginners**
Author: Benjawan Poomsan Becker ©1995
Description: Designed for either self-study or classroom use. Teaches all four language skills— speaking, listening (when used in conjunction with the cassette tapes), reading and writing. Offers clear, easy, step-by-step instruction building on what has been previously learned. Used by many Thai temples and institutes in America.
Cassettes & CD available. Paperback. 268 pages. 6" x 8.5"

Book	US$12.95	Stock # 1001
Three Tape Set	US$20.00	Stock # 1001T
Two CDs	US$20.00	Stock # 1001CD

****

Title: **Lao for Beginners**
Author: Benjawan Poomsan Becker and Buasawan Simmala ©2003
Description: Designed for either self-study or classroom use. Teaches all four language skills— speaking, listening (when used in conjunction with the CDs), reading and writing.
Offers clear, easy, step-by-step instruction building on what has been previously learned.
Cassettes & CDs available. Paperback. 270 pages. 6" x 8.5"

Book	US$12.95	Stock # 1012
Three CDs	US$20.00	Stock # 1012CD

****

Title: **Cambodian for Beginners**
Author: Richard Gilbert and Sovandy Hang ©2004
Description: Designed for either self-study or classroom use. Teaches all four language skills— speaking, listening (when used in conjunction with the CDs), reading and writing .
Offers clear, easy, step-by-step instruction building on what has been previously learned.
CDs available. Paperback. 285 pages. 6" x 8.5"

Book	US$12.95	Stock # 1015
Three CDs	US$20.00	Stock # 1015CD

****

Title:	**Thai for Intermediate Learners**
Author:	Benjawan Poomsan Becker ©1998
Description:	The continuation of *Thai for Beginners*. Users are expected to be able to read basic Thai language. There is transliteration when new words are introduced. Teaches reading, writing and speaking at a higher level. Keeps students interested with cultural facts about Thailand. Helps expand your Thai vocabulary in a systematic way. Two casettes available. Paperback. 220 pages. 6" x 8.5"
Book	US$12.95 Stock # 1002
Two Tape Set	US$15.00 Stock # 1002T

****

Title:	**Thai for Advanced Readers**
Author:	Benjawan Poomsan Becker ©2000
Description:	A book that helps students practice reading Thai at an advanced level. It contains reading exercises, short essays, newspaper articles, cutural and historical facts about Thailand and miscellaneous information about the Thai language. Students need to be able to read basic Thai. Two casettes available. Paperback. 210 pages. 6" x 8.5"
Book	US$12.95 Stock # 1003
Two Tape Set	US$15.00 Stock # 1003T

****

Title:	**Thai for Lovers**
Author:	Nit & Jack Ajee ©1999
Description:	An ideal book for lovers. A short cut to romantic communication in Thailand. There are useful sentences with their Thai translations throughout the book. You won't find any Thai language book more fun and user-friendly. **Rated R!** Two casettes available. Paperback. 190 pages. 6" x 8.5"
Book	US$13.95 Stock #: 1004
Two Tape Set	US$17.00 Stock #: 1004T

****

Title: **Thai-English, English-Thai Dictionary for Non-Thai Speakers**
Author: Benjawan Poomsan Becker ©2002
Description: Designed to help English speakers communicate in Thai. It is equally useful for those who can read the Thai alphabet and those who can't. Most Thai-English dictionaries either use Thai script exclusively for the Thai entries (making them difficult for westerners to use) or use only phonetic transliteration (making it impossible to look up a word in Thai script). This dictionary solves these problems. You will find most of the vocabulary you are likely to need in everyday life, including basic, cultural, political and scientific terms. Paperback. 658 pages. 4.1" x 5.6"
Book US$15.00 Stock # 1010

****

Title: **Lao-English, English-Lao Dictionary for Non-Lao Speakers**
Author: Benjawan Poomsan Becker
Khamphan Mingbuapha ©2003
Description: Designed to help English speakers communicate in Lao. This practical dictionary is useful both in Laos and in Northeast Thailand. Students can use it without having to learn the Lao alphabet. However, there is a comprehensive introduction to the Lao writing system and pronunciation. The transliteration system is the same as that used in Paiboon Publishing's other books. It contains most of the vocabulary used in everyday life, including basic, cultural, political and scientific terms.
Paperback. 780 pages. 4.1" x 5.6"
Book US$15.00 Stock # 1010

****

Title: **Improving Your Thai Pronunciation**
Author: Benjawan Poomsan Becker ©2003
Description: Designed to help foreingers maximize their potential in pronouncing Thai words and enhance their Thai listening and speaking skills. Students will find that they have more confidence in speaking the language and can make themselves understood better. The book and the CDs are made to be used in combination. The course is straight forward, easy to follow and compact.
Paperback. 48 pages. 5" x 7.5" + One-hour CD
Book & CD US$15.00 Stock # 1011

****

Title:	**Thai for Gay Tourists**	
Author:	Saksit Pakdeesiam ©2001	
Description:	The ultimate language guide for gay and bisexual men visiting Thailand. Lots of gay oriented language, culture, commentaries and other information. Instant sentences for convenient use by gay visitors. Fun and sexy. The best way to communicate with your Thai gay friends and partners! **Rated R!** Cassette tapes available. Paperback. 220 pages. 6" x 8.5"	
Book	US$13.95	Stock # 1007
Two Tape Set	US$17.00	Stock # 1007T

****

Title:	**Tai Go No Kiso**	
Author:	Benjawan Poomsan Becker ©2002	
Description:	Thai for Japanese Speakers. Japanese version of "Thai for Beginners". Cassette tapes available. Paperback. 262 pages. 6" x 8.5"	
Book	US$12.95	Stock # 1009
Three Tape Set	US$20.00	Stock # 1009T

****

Deutschsprachiges Lehrbuch über die Thai-Sprache von Paiboon Publishing

Titel:	**Thai für Anfänger**		
Autor:	Benjawan Poomsan Becker ©2000		
Beschreibung:	Für das selbständige Lernen zu Hause oder für den Gebrauch im Klassenzimmer. Vermittelt Grundkenntnisse der Thai-Sprache. Das Buch kann mit den entsprechenden Tonbandkassetten kombiniert werden. Bietet klare und einfache Instruktionen, die Schritt für Schritt auf bereits Erlerntem aufbauen. Wird von zahlreichen Thai Tempeln und Sprachinstituten in Amerika benutzt. Tonbandkassetten erhältlich. Taschenbuch. 245 Seiten. 15 cm x 22 cm		
Buch	US$13.95	Lagernummer	1005
Kassetten (3er Set)	US$20.00	Lagernummer	1005T

****

All books are fun and easy to use.

Mit unseren Büchern macht das Lernen Spass.

THAI-ENGLISH ENGLISH-THAI DICTIONARY FOR PALM OS® PDAS

-- WITH SEARCH-BY-SOUND™ --

Travelling to Thailand? Learning the Thai Language? Imagine having instant access to 21,000 English, Phonetic, and Thai words right on your Palm OS® PDA, with large, clear fonts and everyday vocabulary. If you're not familiar with the Thai alphabet, you can also look up Thai words by their sound. Perfect for the casual traveller or the dedicated Thai learner.

This Thai-English English-Thai Dictionary for Palm OS® PDAs...

❒ is software which runs on Palm OS® PDAs.
❒ has approximately 21,000 words (about 9,000 English, 6,000 phonetic and 6,000 Thai).
❒ has four crisp font sizes.
❒ is useful for people who know the Thai alphabet and those who don't.
❒ has three sections - just like the paper dictionary.
❒ can be used to look up a word by its "sound" without knowing the Thai alphabet.
❒ supports all Palm OS® devices with Palm OS® 3.5 or greater, including devices from Palm, Inc., Handspring, Sony, IBM, and Kyocera.
❒ has a convenient, optional on-screen keyboard for entering English, Phonetic, and Thai
❒ is completely standalone: does not require "Thai enablers" or any other third-party software.
❒ is fast for searching words: usually only need to tap in a few letters of your word.
❒ takes advantage of high-density Palm OS® devices by providing extra-crisp fonts.
❒ is very user-friendly.

Available by download or CD-ROM. Please check for prices on our web site at www.paiboonpublishing.com.

PAIBOON PUBLISHING

ORDER FORM

QTY.	ITEM NO.	NAME OF ITEM	ITEM PRICE	TOTAL

Delivery Charges for First Class and Airmail

	USA and Canada	**Other Countries**
Up to $25.00	US$3.95	US$8.95
$25.01-$50.00	US$4.95	US$11.95
$50.01-$75.00	US$6.25	US$15.25
$75.01-$100.00	US$7.75	US$18.75
Over $100.00	FREE	US$18.75

Merchandise Total	
CA residents add 8.25% sales tax	
Delivery Charge (See chart at left)	
Total	

Method of Payment ❒ Check ❒ Money Order Make payable to Paiboon Publishing
Charge to: ❒ Visa ❒ Master Card

Card # ______________________ Exp. Date ____/____

Signature______________________ Tel ______________

Name ______________________ Date ______________

Address ______________________________________

____

____

Email Address ______________________________________

Mail order is for orders outside of Thailand only.
Send your order and payment to: Paiboon Publishing
PMB 192, 1442A Walnut Street, Berkeley, CA 94709 USA
Tel: 1-510-848-7086 Fax: 1-510-848-4521
orders@paiboonpublishing.com
www.paiboonpublishing.com
Allow 2-3 weeks for delivery.

PAIBOON PUBLISHING

Printed by Chulalongkorn University Printing House Thailand
June 2004 4708-237/5,000(4)
http://www.cuprint.chula.ac.th